REALLY funny

DOCTOR! DOCTOR!

jokes....

Mickey MacIntyre

The Really Funny...
DOCTOR! DOCTOR! Joke Book For Kids.
Over 200 side-splitting, rib-tickling jokes that are
guaranteed to keep the doctor at bay!

Mickey MacIntyre

ISBN 978-1-909855-32-8

Contents

the REALLY funny....

4

Top Ten Tips For Telling Jokes

Practice, Practice, Practice!

Know your joke. Ok so it's only a short Doctor! Doctor! joke, but mess it up and no one will be laughing. Make sure you know your joke 'off by heart' and practice it in front of a mirror. Learning your lines means you can concentrate on 'telling' the joke instead of just reading it.

Know when to be quiet! Don't start explaining the joke the second you have told it. Let your audience work it out for a few seconds and they will laugh when they 'get' it.

Don't tell jokes that could get you in trouble.

Avoid subjects that might fall into this category like rude or insensitive jokes. All the jokes in The REALLY Funny Doctor! Doctor! Joke Book are clean

DOCTOR! DOCTOR! joke book for kids

and trouble free!

Don't announce you are about to tell a joke. Your audience is more likely to find a joke funny if they don't have a big announcement that they are about to hear something 'REALLY FUNNY'.

Don't tell everyone how funny your joke is before you tell it. It makes your audience expect too much.

Don't laugh at your own jokes until your audience has laughed. Give your audience time to 'get' the joke. Most of the best joke tellers tell their jokes with a 'straight' face.

the REALLY funny....

Choose your moment. There are bad times to tell a joke. For example if someone is really busy or sick, sad or has hurt themselves. Pick a time when everyone is in a good mood and wants to have some fun.

Take your time. Don't rush. Speeding through words too quickly will make it difficult to understand and if you have to repeat a joke, it's not as funny.

Speak clearly and make sure you 'get' the joke before you tell it. Think about the way the punch line should sound and practice it. If you think it's funny someone else will too!

Study your favourite comedians or anyone else you see on TV or youtube. Watch how they 'work' the audience, how they deliver their punch lines, what they do with their hands. Learn from the professionals!!

We hope you enjoy reading and telling our 'Doctor! Doctor!' jokes and hopefully are inspired to write a few of your own.

Enjoy!

the **REALLY** funny....

.....now for the **REALLY** funny DOCTOR! DOCTOR! jokes....

Doctor, doctor! I'm frightened of squirrels.
You must be nuts!

Doctor, doctor! I keep thinking I'm a rubber band.
Well, perhaps you are over-stretching yourself!

Doctor, doctor! You've got to help me - I just can't stop my hands shaking!
Did you drink a lot?
Not really - most of it spilled out!

Doctor, doctor! I think I'm shrinking.
Well take these tablets but you'll have to be a little patient!

the **REALLY** funny....

Doctor, doctor! I think I need glasses.
You certainly do Sir, this is a fish and chip shop!

Doctor, doctor! I think I'm suffering from Deja Vu!
Didn't I see you yesterday?

Doctor, doctor! Whenever I talk, people ignore me.
Next please!

Doctor, doctor! My sister thinks she's a car!
Well, show her in at once.
I can't - she's run out of petrol down the road!

Doctor, doctor! I keep thinking I'm a pair of curtains.
Pull yourself together!

Doctor, doctor! I keep thinking I'm a bee.
Buzz off! Can't you see I'm busy?

Doctor, doctor! I keep thinking I'm a mosquito.
Go away, sucker!

Doctor, doctor! I keep thinking I'm a goat.
And how long has this been going on?
Oh, ever since I was a kid!

Doctor, doctor! I keep stealing things.
Have you taken anything for it?

Doctor, doctor! I can't get to sleep.
Lie on the edge of the bed and you'll soon drop off!

Doctor, doctor! I feel like a king.
What's your name?
Joe.
You must be Joe King!

Doctor, doctor! I tend to flush a lot.
Don't worry it's just a chain reaction!

Doctor, doctor! There's a man here who says he's turning invisible!
Tell him I can't see him just now!

Doctor, doctor! I think I'm a worm!
Well just wriggle onto the chair!

Doctor, doctor! I keep seeing pink and yellow elephants!
Have you seen the psychiatrist?
No only pink and yellow elephants!

Doctor, doctor! I keep thinking I'm a frog!
What's wrong with that?
I think I'm going to croak!

Doctor, doctor! Please hurry, my son swallowed a razor-blade.
Don't panic, I'm coming immediately.
Have you done anything yet?
Yeah, I shaved with the electric razor!

Doctor, doctor! I feel like a carrot.
Don't get yourself in a stew!

Doctor, doctor! My baby's swallowed a bullet.
Well, don't point him at anyone until I get there!

Doctor, doctor! I'm convinced I'm a rubber band.
Why don't you stretch yourself out on the couch over there and tell me all about it!

Doctor, doctor! They've dropped me from the cricket team- they call me butterfingers.
Don't worry, what you have is not catching!

Doctor, doctor! I keep dreaming there are great, gooey, bug-eyed monsters playing tiddlywinks under my bed. What shall I do?
Hide the tiddlywinks!

Doctor, doctor! I keep thinking I'm the Abominable Snowman. Sorry, I don't get your drift!

Doctor, doctor! A crate of eggs fell on my head!
Well, the yolk's on you!

Doctor, doctor! I feel like a billiard ball.
Well get to the back of the queue!

Doctor, doctor! I keep painting myself gold.
Don't worry it's just a gilt complex!

Doctor, doctor! I keep thinking I'm a caterpillar.
Don't worry you'll soon change!

Doctor, doctor! I've got a problem with my waterworks.
Have you seen any plumbers?

Doctor, doctor! I feel like a bridge!
Oh dear, what's come over you?
So far, 2 lorries and 5 cars!

Doctor, doctor! I've a pain at the base of my back.
Let's get to the bottom of this!

Doctor, doctor! I think I'm a wasp
Buzz off then!

Doctor, doctor! I feel so tired, I don't
know where I am half the time.
Open wide now!

Doctor, doctor! My daughter
thinks she's an actress.
Don't worry - it's just a stage
she's going through!

Doctor, doctor! I just swallowed a mouth
organ.
Think yourself lucky you don't play the
piano!

Doctor, doctor! I keep thinking I'm in a jazz band.
Stop blowing your own trumpet!

Doctor, doctor! I'm in love with the king of the vampires.
That sounds like a royal pain in the neck!

Doctor, doctor! I think there's a slight imbalance between potassium and sodium ions inside my body!
Are you sure?
Yes, I'm positive!

Doctor, doctor! I keep hearing a ringing sound!
Try answering the phone!

the REALLY funny....

Doctor, doctor! My father thinks he's a tree.
We'd better nip this in the bud!

Doctor, doctor! I can see the future!
When did this start happening?
Next Tuesday!

Doctor, doctor! What's wrong with me?
Well, you've got a carrot up your nose, a bean in one ear and a French fry in the other. I'd say you're not eating right!

Doctor, doctor! What should I do if my temperature goes up a point or more?
Sell!

Doctor, doctor! Every night my foot falls asleep.
What's wrong with that?
It snores!

Doctor, doctor! I think I'm a computer.
Hold on, I'll just connect you to the internet!

Doctor, doctor! I'm addicted to crossword puzzles.
Try not to get too down.
Two down, are you kidding me?
That's easier than five across!

Doctor, doctor! I think I'm a kleptomaniac.
Take one of these pills three times a day,
and if that doesn't work get me a new
iPad please!

Doctor, doctor! What should I do I get sick
while traveling?
Try sitting in a different part of the bus!

Doctor, doctor! I keep seeing double.
Sit down on the couch.
Which one?

Doctor, doctor! I keep thinking I'm a dog
Take a seat!
I can't. I'm not allowed on the furniture!

Doctor, doctor! Will I be able to play the violin after the operation?
Yes, of course.
Great! I never could before!

Doctor, doctor! I think I'm a bell.
Take these and if it doesn't help give me a ring!

Doctor, doctor! Have you got something for a bad headache?
Of course. Just take this hammer and hit yourself on the head. Then you'll have a really bad headache!

Doctor, doctor! I've got terrible wind. Is there anything you can give me?
Yes-have my kite!

Doctor, doctor! I've swallowed a bone!
Are you choking?
No, really I did!

Doctor, doctor! Can I have a second opinion?
Of course, come back tomorrow!

Doctor, doctor! I think I'm a moth.
So why did you come around then?
Well, I saw this light at the window!

Doctor, doctor! I've just swallowed a clock! Don't worry - there's no cause for alarm!

Doctor, doctor! I feel like a dog.
How long have you felt like this?
Since, I was a puppy!

Doctor, doctor! I'm having this terrible memory problem!
How long have you been having this problem?
Problem, what problem?

Doctor, doctor! I've a carrot growing in my ear.
How did that happen?
I don't know - I planted cauliflowers!

Doctor, doctor! I've swallowed my pocket money.
Take this and we'll see if there's any change in the morning!

Doctor, doctor! I keep thinking I'm a vampire.
Necks, please!

Doctor, doctor! I've got bad teeth, foul breath and smelly feet.
Sounds like you've got foot and mouth disease!

Doctor, doctor! I have a ringing in my ears! What should I do?
Get an unlisted number!

Doctor, doctor! I feel like a £10 note.
Go shopping, the change will do you good!

Doctor, doctor! I think I'm a yo-yo.
Are you stringing me along!

the REALLY funny....

Doctor, doctor! I keep thinking I'm a spider.
What a web of lies!

Doctor doctor! I think I'm spending too much time on the computer, I'm starting to see spots in front of my eyes.
Have you seen an optician?
No, just spots!

Doctor, doctor! A bee stung me. Can you put some ointment on it?
No, it'll be long gone by now!

Doctor, doctor! I have 2 big toes on my right foot and 2 little toes on my left foot.
You must have Mix-ama-toe-sis!

Doctor, doctor! I keep losing my memory.
When did you first notice that?
When did I first notice what?

Doctor, doctor! My eleven-year-old son weighs fifteen stone and is seven feet tall.
Don't worry - he'll grow out of it!

Doctor, doctor! What did the x-ray of my head show?
Absolutely nothing!

Doctor, doctor! I've swallowed a quilt.
I thought you looked a bit down in the mouth!

Doctor, doctor! I'm allergic to the high jump.
Don't worry - you'll soon get over it!

Doctor, doctor! I feel like a sewing machine.
Don't tell everyone or they'll all try and stitch you up!

Doctor, doctor! There's something wrong with my hearing.
What are the symptoms?
They're a yellow cartoon family on tv!

Doctor, doctor! I feel like I'm turning into a bear!
How long have you felt this way?
Ever since, I was a cub!

Doctor, doctor! Everyone tries to take advantage of me. What should I do?
Give me £200 and let me borrow your car!

Doctor, doctor! I've got a terribly sore throat.
Go over to the window and stick your tongue out.
Will that cure it?
No, I just don't like my neighbour!

Doctor, doctor! I swallowed a cantaloupe.
You'll be feeling very melon-choly then!

Doctor, doctor! Help me. My teenage son thinks he's a refrigerator.
Stay calm. I'm sure he'll chill out!

Doctor, doctor! I feel like a dog.
Then, go and see a vet!

Doctor, doctor! I keep dreaming I'm being thrown at a giant, bug-eyed monster, who keeps dropping me
Don't worry - it's not catching!

Doctor, doctor! I feel like a bucket.
You do look a little pail!

Doctor, doctor! Please do the operation safely. This is my first operation.
It's my first operation too!

Doctor, doctor! I keep on thinking I'm a frog.
What's wrong with that?
I'm worried that I might croak!

Doctor, doctor! I keep thinking I'm a needle!
Hmmmm well I see your point!

Doctor, doctor! I feel like a sheep.
That's baaaaaaaaad!

Doctor, doctor! I feel like biscuits!
What, you mean those square ones?
Yes!
The ones you put butter on?
Yes!
Oh, You're crackers!

Doctor, doctor! Should I file my nails?
No, throw them away like everybody else!

Doctor, doctor! I keep snoring so loudly I wake myself up.
Sleep in another room then!

Doctor, doctor! I keep thinking I'm a jeweller.
Take this pill and then give me a ring!

Doctor, doctor! I feel like a race horse.
Take one of these every 4 laps!

Doctor, doctor! I keep thinking there's two of me
One at a time please!

Doctor, doctor! I feel run down.
Well look both ways before crossing the road next time!

Doctor, doctor! I keep thinking
I'm a nit.
Will you get out of my hair!

Doctor, doctor! What happened to that man who fell into the circular saw and had the whole left side of his body cut away? He's all right now!

Doctor, doctor! I've got acute appendicitis.
You've got a cute smile too!

Doctor, doctor! I keep thinking I'm a bin.
Don't talk such rubbish!

Doctor, doctor! I keep thinking I'm a clock.
OK, just relax. There's no need to get yourself wound up!

Doctor, doctor! I dream there are monsters under my bed, what can I do?
Saw the legs off of your bed!

Doctor, doctor! I keep thinking I'm a woodworm.
How boring for you!

Doctor, doctor! I can't pronounce my F's, T's and H's,
Well you can't say fairer than that then!

Doctor, doctor! I think I'm Scooby Doo.
Here's a prescription for a Scooby snack!

Doctor, doctor! What do you give an injured lemon?
Lemonade!

Doctor, doctor! I'm so ugly what can I do about it?
Hire yourself out for Halloween parties!

Doctor, doctor! I've swallowed some uranium.
You've probably got atomic-ache!

Doctor, doctor! I can't stop playing Scrabble.
My word!

Doctor, doctor! I feel like a pair of trunks".
Relax man and go for a swim!

Doctor, doctor! My uncle thinks he's a
tube of glue.
He must be losing his grip on reality!

Doctor, doctor! I've broken my leg. What
shall I do?
Limp!

Doctor, doctor! I'm allergic to
perfume.
I'll have you scent to a
specialist!

Doctor, doctor! I have yellow teeth, what do I do?
Wear a brown tie!

Doctor, doctor! Will you treat me?
No, you'll have to pay like everyone else!

Doctor, doctor! I keep thinking I'm a stand-up comedian.
Have you tried playing some shows?
No - will it cure me?
Of course - laughter's the best medicine!

Doctor, doctor! I feel like a cup of tea.
What's got into you?
Milk and two sugars!

Doctor, doctor! I can't breathe perfectly.
Don't worry, I will stop that permanently!

Doctor, doctor! When I press with my finger here... it hurts, and here... it hurts, and here... and here... What do you think is wrong with me?
You have a broken finger!

Doctor, doctor! My brother thinks he's a lift.
Why didn't he come in?
He doesn't stop at this floor!

Doctor, doctor! I think I'm an electric eel.
That's shocking!

Doctor, doctor! Is there anything wrong
with my heart?
After a thorough examination I can
confidently say it will last as long as you
do!

Doctor, doctor! Nobody understands me.
What do you mean by that?

Doctor, doctor! My sister here keeps
thinking she's invisible!
What sister?

Doctor, doctor! I keep thinking I'm a fruitcake.

What's got into you?

Flour, butter, raisins - all the usual ingredients!

Doctor, doctor! I couldn't drink my medicine after my bath like you told me

Why not?

Well after I'd drunk my bath I didn't have room for the medicine!

Doctor, doctor! My nose runs and feet smell.

Oh no! I think you might have been built upside down!

Doctor, doctor! I'm always talking to myself.
I shouldn't worry about that.
But I'm so boring!

Doctor, doctor! I feel funny today. What should I do?
Become a comedian!

Doctor, doctor! I've had tummy ache since I ate three crabs yesterday.
Did they smell bad when you took them out of their shells?
What do you mean took them out of their shells!

Doctor, doctor! It hurts when
I do this.
Then don't do that!

Doctor, doctor! I think I'm a guitar.
Don't pull my strings!

Doctor, doctor! I woke up this morning to
find a banana, an orange, some grapes,
and some ice cream in my ears.
You're just a trifle deaf!

Doctor, doctor! My aunt has a sore throat.
Give her this bottle of auntie-septic!

Doctor, doctor! I think I'm suffering from hallucinations.
I'm sure you're just imagining it!

Doctor, doctor! I just can't keep track of time.
I can see that - your appointment isn't until next Tuesday!

Doctor, doctor! Was the pain in my back a slipped disc?
No, twisted braces!

Doctor, doctor! My feet have grown to three times their normal size and my nose has swelled up and gone red
Aw, come on now - stop clowning around!

Doctor, doctor! Can you help me out?
Of course, the exit is just over there!

Doctor, doctor! Have you got
anything for my liver?
What about some onions?

Doctor, doctor! My little boy has just
swallowed a roll of film.
Well let's just wait and see if anything
develops!

Doctor, doctor! How do I stop my nose
from running?
Stick your foot out and trip it up!

Doctor, doctor! I'm boiling up.
Just simmer down please!

Doctor, doctor! I think I
swallowed a pillow.
How do you feel?
A little down in the mouth!

Doctor, doctor! You know those pills you
gave me for my stomach?
What about them?
They keep rolling off in the middle of the
night!

Doctor, doctor! I'm on a diet and it's
making me really irritable, yesterday I bit
someone's ear off.
Oh dear, that's a lot of calories!

Doctor, doctor! I feel like a bird.
Perch over there, I'll tweet you
in a minute!

Doctor, doctor! I keep thinking I'm a snake
about to shed its skin.
Why don't you go behind the screen and
slip into something more comfortable
then!

Doctor, doctor! What's the quickest way
to get to hospital?
Lie in the road outside!

Doctor, doctor! I've a strawberry stuck in
my ear!
Don't worry, I've some cream for that!

Doctor, doctor! I've a split personality
Well, you'd better both sit down then!

Doctor, doctor! I keep thinking I'm in an lift with a monster.
You may be coming down with something!

Doctor, doctor! My head is splitting.
Let me axe you one or two questions!

Doctor, doctor! I think everyone hates me.
Don't be stupid, not everyone has met you yet!

Doctor, doctor! Is there anything you can give me for bad wind?
Have you tried an air freshener?

Doctor, doctor! What are my chances of losing weight?
Slim, madam!

Doctor, doctor! I keep thinking I'm still at school.
Sit down over there and I'll exam-ine you!

Doctor, doctor! There's a man in the waiting room with a glass eye named Brown.
What does he call his other eye?

Doctor, doctor! I feel like a spoon!
Ok. Sit still and don't stir too much!

Doctor, doctor! Every time I drink tea my eye hurts.
Try taking the teaspoon out of the cup first!

Doctor, doctor! You have to help me out.
Of course, which way do you want to go?

Doctor, doctor! How is that boy who swallowed a penny?
No change yet!

Doctor, doctor! Every single bone in my body is broken.
Well, I hope you can get your money back!

Doctor, doctor! I'm scared of cats.
I've got the purrfect cure for you!

Doctor, doctor! I've only got 59 seconds to live.
Just wait a minute will you!

Doctor, doctor! I'm scared of Father Christmas.
You're suffering from Claus-trophobia!

Doctor, doctor! I've just eaten 25 pancakes, or was it 26? No, it was 27 pancakes.
Stop this waffling!

Doctor, doctor! My hair keeps falling out! What should I do?
Here's a jar to keep it in!

Doctor, doctor! My hearing aid isn't working.
What's wrong with it?
Half past nine!

Doctor, doctor! People keep disagreeing with me.
No, they don't!

Doctor, doctor! If I take these pills, will I get better?
Well no one has ever come back for more!

Doctor, doctor! I'm not getting much sleep.
Have you tried counting sheep?
Yes, and that's the problem. The nearest farm is miles away and it's morning by the time I get home!

Doctor, doctor! I feel like a window.
Tell me where the pane is!

Doctor, doctor! Do you think strawberries are healthy?
I've never heard one complain!

Doctor, doctor! I've just swallowed a pen. Well sit down and write your name!

Doctor, doctor! Will you give me something for my head? Erm no sorry, I don't need a spare but thanks anyway!

Doctor, doctor! Will this ointment clear up my spots? It might but I can't make rash promises!

Doctor, doctor! My son swallowed my pen, what should I do? Use a pencil till I get there!

Doctor, doctor! I keep thinking I'm invisible.
Who said that?

Doctor, doctor! You said I'd be dead in ten - ten what? Years? Months?
10, 9, 8, 7, 6...

Doctor, doctor! Aaa, Eee, I, ooh! You... I think you may have terrible vowel syndrome!

Doctor, doctor! I'm a burglar!
Have you taken anything for it?

Doctor, doctor! My mind keeps wandering.
Don't worry - it's too weak to go very far!

Doctor, doctor! I'm afraid of the dark.
Then, leave the light on!

Doctor, doctor! Is it true what they say: that an apple a day keeps the doctor away?
At first, then after a while we get good at dodging them!

Doctor, doctor! Every time I eat fruit I get this strange urge to give people all my money.
Would you like an apple or a banana?

Doctor, doctor! You've taken out my tonsils, my adenoids, my gall bladder, my varicose veins and my appendix, but I still don't feel well.
That's quite enough out of you!

Doctor, doctor! There's a spinning fly following me.
Don't worry it's just a bug that's going around!

Doctor, doctor! I can't see!
Open your eyes then!

Doctor, doctor! I've got amnesia.
Just go home and try to forget about it!

Doctor, doctor! I keep comparing things with something else.
Don't worry, it's only an-alogy!

Doctor, doctor! Sorry I'm late, I broke my ankle.
Huh - another lame excuse!

Doctor, doctor! What's the best way to avoid biting insects?
Don't bite any!

Doctor, doctor! What do you charge for treating a split personality?
£15 each!

Doctor, doctor! Can you help me? My tongue keeps sticking out.

That's good. Now, if you can just lick these stamps!

Doctor, doctor! How can I cure my sleep-walking?

Easy. Just sprinkle drawing pins on your bedroom floor!

Doctor, doctor! I think I'm a snail.

Don't worry we'll soon have you out of your shell!

Doctor, doctor! I keep thinking I'm a duck.

Why don't you try a quack doctor?

Doctor, doctor! I think I'm an Accountant.
You'd better work on your balance!

Doctor, doctor! I can't stop auditioning
people - is there anything you can do for
me?
How about a little tap dance? Or maybe I
could do a song?

Doctor, doctor! I feel like a pack of cards.
I'll deal with you later!

Doctor, doctor! Everyone thinks I'm a liar.
I find that hard to believe!

Doctor, doctor! I can't stop trembling.
I'll be with you in a couple of shakes!

Doctor, doctor! What do you recommend for flat feet?
Try a foot pump!

Doctor, doctor! I have a big problem: my nose hair won't stop growing.
How long have you had it?
About three metres so far!

Doctor, doctor! I'm half dead.
Don't worry I'll bury you up to your waist!

Doctor, doctor! I've developed a double heartbeat since my operation.
Ah, so that's where my wristwatch went!

Doctor, doctor! What's the best way to stop my nose running?
Stand on your head!

Doctor, doctor! I keep thinking I'm a piece of carpet
Well, stop letting people walk all over you!

Doctor, doctor! When I get up in the morning, I'm always dizzy for half an hour.
Try getting up half an hour later!

Doctor, doctor! I feel as if everyone and everything is up against me.
Would it help if we moved to a bigger surgery?

the REALLY funny....

More REALLY Funny Joke Books

You may also enjoy
**'The REALLY Funny
Knock! Knock! Joke
Book For Kids'.**

And

**'The REALLY Funny
LOL! Joke Book
For Kids'.**

Plus look out for more **REALLY
Funny** joke books from **Mickey
MacIntyre** coming soon. Just
search Mickey MacIntyre on
Amazon.

Printed in Great Britain
by Amazon.co.uk, Ltd.,
Marston Gate.